Getting the Big Scholarships

Learn Expert Secrets for
Winning College Cash!

Lee Binz,

The HomeScholar

First Printing, 2018

Printed in the United States of America

Cover Design by Robin Montoya
Edited by Kimberly Charron

ISBN: 1983427896
ISBN-13: 978-1983427893

Getting the Big Scholarships

Learn Expert Secrets for Winning College Cash!

Introduction

Relief from Homeschool Parent Night Terrors

Remember when you fell in love with your baby? Remember when you loved homeschooling? Your child was young and enthusiastic, and each year was a new adventure. When my children were young, I knew college was out there but it seemed like a long way away. We were single income with some retirement savings but mostly spent on life, and college savings were something for *tomorrow*. My head was in the sand. College seemed so far off!

My boys were about two years apart. Naturally, we thought our college expenses would be spread out over six years. When our eldest was in 9th grade, it dawned on us that Alex (our youngest) had caught up academically with Kevin (our eldest). We started to realize they would graduate at the same time and attend college at the same time. Doing the math, we eventually figured out that rather than expenses spread out over *six* years they would be over *four* years. This was coupled with the fact that by middle school we hadn't saved anything for college. In fact, we chose family over finances by deciding to move closer to grandparents who lived in an expensive neighborhood instead of saving that money for college.

I know where you are—at the beginning of a rapidly-rising panic attack. For me, I think full panic set in when our financial planner said we should have been saving for college at a rate of $300 per child per month since birth. Since we had managed to overlook the first 15 years of saving, that number had grown to astronomical levels. My husband is a trained project manager and we both have an aversion to debt so we decided we had three choices.

1. Just say *no* to college.

2. I would go back to work full time as an RN and work their way through college.

3. Try to win two full scholarships.

I decided to go with option three and started researching how to get scholarships, paying attention to all the crazy details and ideas out there.

I became obsessed with keeping high school records and presenting them to get the best scholarships. We decided to play to our strengths. The problem was, our kids were academic - they did not excel in sports and had nowhere near the volunteer hours they needed. They weren't overly social, only sweet, ordinary, loveable, nerdy guys, but with some interesting and unusual passions (chess and economics).

We decided our best play in this desperate situation was to let them go all out on their passions and we would fall in behind and try to document everything they did in a way that would demand colleges' attention. It became a necessity to put together the *best* homeschool records I could to have any chance for our kids to achieve their dreams.

Flash forward a few years, with my husband and I staring at each other in shocked disbelief after one phone call. We'd found out that our modest piggy bank was *saved*. *Both* our boys had won *full tuition scholarships* from their first choice university. Our investment in record keeping had worked!

In the beginning, college had seemed like a dream for one, let alone two children. I was looking at working for 10 years as a nurse (and going back to college myself, so I could work again). Instead, our kids could now go to college and emerge debt-free. Their combined scholarships amounted to over $184,000—money we didn't have, keeping our piggy bank intact after all our worries. That's what scholarships can do for your family! I took what I'd learned and started my business to help other homeschool parents.

Most homeschool families I know have not saved up enough money to pay for their children's college education, and are relying on scholarship money to help defray costs. But what if you knew there were concrete ways to increase the odds of your child receiving scholarships? Wouldn't you want to learn all about these tips and start to work on them right away?

That's why I wrote this e-book, so you too will have the information you need to help your children succeed and win big scholarships. I'm sure that if a regular family like ours can earn great scholarships, then almost anyone can with the right tools and information. In my work as a homeschool consultant, I've helped thousands of parents across the country position their children to earn college scholarships, so I know it's possible!

Of course, merely reading an e-book won't make your child win fabulous scholarships! But the information here will give you an overview of everything that goes into preparing your child for success. This is a place to start without being overwhelmed, so read the information here and then start to implement it over time. If you combine it with the many other resources I offer on my website, you'll learn what you need to know to achieve scholarship success.

Chapter 1

Three Kinds of College Scholarships

There are three kinds of college scholarships:

1. Need-based Financial Aid

Need-based financial aid is related to the FAFSA that you fill out for the first time in October of senior year. FAFSA stands for Free Application for Federal Student Aid. This application will help the federal government decide how much they think you can afford to pay for college each year.

The U.S. Department of Education requires the FAFSA to receive any government money for college, such as grants and loans. This form is how the

15

government conducts a need analysis with information from your income tax forms, which determines your Expected Family Contribution (EFC)—how much the government thinks you can afford.

Awards are given as grants and loans. Loans must be repaid. These may include work study, such as work in the school cafeteria, which doesn't usually pay well. These scholarships are first come, first served.

There may not be much help for middle income families because the government figures out how much money you deserve. Still, it's worthwhile to try. In my family, we could have received $2500.

2. Private Aid

Businesses and organizations often offer private aid. Search for scholarship opportunities awarded for special talents or abilities and complete the applications, which often include a written essay or project along with the submission of thorough homeschool records.

There are many unused scholarships out there, with awards varying in amount. As your child completes applications and essays for these scholarships, you can use the work for high school English credit. For more information, read my coffee break book, *College Scholarships for High School Credit*. This can save you quite a bit of money on an English curriculum. But there is no guarantee of success, even if your child applies for a million private scholarships.

Here is my suggested process to follow to find suitable private scholarships for your child.

1. Find scholarships. Try using collegenet.com or fastweb.com.

2. Filter out the ones that don't fit your child, using the mantra, "One strike and you're out."

3. File them, so they are arranged by due date.

4. Follow-through is up to the student, so allow time for essay writing, project creation, and the application.

Keep in mind that you can reuse these essays for other scholarship and college applications.

We worked hard at these scholarship opportunities. My boys submitted one scholarship application per week, and each earned about $2500, which we were thrilled about. However, it was only enough to pay for books and fees, and not much more. Private scholarships won't earn big scholarships for most students.

3. Merit-based Scholarships

Students receive merit-based scholarships directly from colleges when they apply. These can be automatically awarded, based on SAT or ACT scores, or GPA. Therefore, it's incredibly important to provide grades, so your child has a GPA on which to base scholarships and to make sure your child has excellent test scores or other outside documentation, to demonstrate their GPA is well-earned. Colleges may also give scholarships related to special skills or talents. If your son plays first base on the baseball team and a college needs a first baseman, they may be willing to give a full tuition scholarship. A merit scholarship might be awarded due to special musical ability, or a special talent in academics.

Merit scholarships might be based on something your child has accomplished, such as volunteer work or working in the Civil Air Patrol. Or it can be based on a future plan, such as the commitment to engage in military service in the future.

Degree-related scholarships are also available, especially for in-demand fields such as engineering, nursing, or teaching. If your child says, "I don't have a clue what I want to do, but I'm pretty good at math and science," they could choose degree-related scholarship areas such as engineering or nursing.

Some organizations give merit-based scholarships based on unique qualities. One of our sons earned a merit-based scholarship simply because he was part Italian! He didn't have to do anything to earn it but be who he was! If your child meets a certain criterion, they might win scholarship money. And criteria are as wide and varied as people are different.

Merit-based scholarships are the most lucrative kind of scholarship, so this book is devoted to helping you get these big scholarships. Our children received scholarships to every college where they applied, and were given over $184,000 in full-tuition scholarships to our first choice college. They even got a matching award from our second choice college!

You must *convince* colleges your child

has something worthy of a merit scholarship. How? Through what I like to call "clipping college coupons"—doing all the trivial things that added together will create incentive for colleges to give your child enormous financial awards, such as:

- Providing a rigorous education – core classes and more
- Including genuine activities and volunteer work – the extra-curriculars that demonstrate true interests
- Preparing a professional and accurate transcript and thorough course descriptions – so they can check your homeschool's academic rigor
- Meaningful college visits – so the details used can be used in the application process
- Timely completion of admission forms – these are inflexible deadlines
- Great letters of recommendation – from people outside your family

- Self-reflective, technically perfect college application essays written by your teenager

Chapter 2

Planning High School Courses

The most important way to prepare your child to earn merit-based scholarships is to plan a rigorous curriculum, whether your child is trying for an academic scholarship or not. If a college needs a first baseman and two excellent candidates apply, the school will choose the first baseman who has also studied a rigorous curriculum. Providing a rigorous curriculum for your children ensures all their eggs aren't in only one talent basket!

Exceed the Suggestions

A typical college prep plan for homeschool high school includes four years of English, math, and social studies (including world history, U.S. history, economics, and government), and three years of science (one lab science). Colleges want to see two or three years of a single foreign language, two years of P.E., and one or more years of fine arts, with electives that add up to 24 or more for regular college prep.

When your family needs a big scholarship, it becomes important to exceed the regular college prep plan and include more intense classes, plus AP or CLEP exams. Whatever you do, make sure you cover all areas. Try to exceed the maximum requirements when you can.

Let's take the example of the first baseman above. This student will make sure to cover the suggested four years of English, math, and social studies, but also four years of science (beyond the suggested minimum of three), and may have six credits of P.E. due to playing baseball and swimming during the same year.

When we homeschooled, there were certain areas in which we could exceed the requirements without making it seem like hard work. For instance, my children loved social sciences. My youngest son, Alex, racked up about six or seven credits in economics! Alex exceeded the recommended social studies credits because he studied economics all the time for fun. He also exceeded the single fine arts credit because he took piano every year.

Too Many Credits?

It's not unusual for homeschool kids to end up with 35 or more credits by the time they graduate, particularly if they are getting credit in their passions and areas in which they're gifted. Although your local public high school may state, "high school graduation for college prep is 22 to 24 credits," some kids have more. Merely because your child has earned the required number of credits to graduate, doesn't mean you must graduate them right then. This is one of the advantages of homeschooling—you get to decide what works best for your family.

Chapter 3

The SAT, ACT, and Outside Documentation

For homeschoolers who want to win big scholarships (and who doesn't), one of the most important steps to success is to provide some outside documentation of your student's abilities. Colleges can be skeptical of grades from any school (not only from a homeschool). They are worried about grade inflation from public schools and private schools alike. They see the overall quality of education decreasing while student's grade point averages seem to be going up. They see large numbers of students coming in as freshmen who don't know how to write!

Colleges want to know what students have learned before they come to college, and they want to know if students are likely to succeed academically before they invest scholarship money in a student. That's why it's helpful to provide some outside documentation, to substantiate your mommy credits and grades. One of the best ways to substantiate your student's academic abilities is through college admission tests such as the SAT and the ACT, which is one of the reasons colleges require these tests. SAT tests measure reading, writing, and math, and the ACT also measures science, so these are excellent ways to provide outside documentation in these subject areas.

One of the best things your student can do to earn a big scholarship is to study hard for the SAT or the ACT. First, it's important to find out which test your student should focus on. You'll find sample tests for both the SAT and ACT at HomeHighSchoolHelp.com. Give your child a sample test in each one and compare their scores to see which one makes them look like a genius. Your child can take the test that presents them in the best possible light, so it's important to try a sample of each, to determine which one shows your student's strengths. Many students perform better on one test over the other, so figure out which works best for your student.

The best way to get scholarship money is to raise your child's scores as much as possible. Some colleges publish in their brochures exactly how much money each score on the SAT is worth to them. For instance, "If you have a 550 on each section of the SAT, we'll give you five thousand a year. And if you have a 650 on each section of the SAT, we'll give you eight thousand a year. And if you have a 750 or better on the SAT, we'll give you twelve thousand per year." Multiply these amounts by four. Simply by studying, your child could essentially earn forty-eight thousand dollars a year toward college! It is a big deal.

It's important to remember that colleges are businesses, and their business is rated by their students' SAT and ACT test scores. Businesses have a stock market price, and the stock market value goes up or down. They will do better if it goes up, and worse when it goes down. Colleges are like this, too. If their average SAT scores go up, their business is rated higher. If their average SAT scores go down, then their business is rated lower. Make sure your student's personal SAT score will bring the college's average up. When your student's test scores are higher than the college's average, they want to pay money to attract them to their college to raise their average students' SAT or ACT scores.

How to Study for the SAT or ACT

Studying for the SAT and the ACT can be done in several ways. Our sons studied for the SAT three days a week during their last two years of high school. They took the test, I timed it, then they corrected it themselves and reviewed their answers for anything incorrect. This raised their test scores almost 200 points per section on the SAT. They started slightly above average and ended up close to perfect. I recommend the books, 9 *Practice Tests for the SAT* and *Cracking the ACT* by Princeton Review, which both include practice tests.

Different kids study effectively in diverse ways. If your child can work hard and is relatively compliant, then studying for the SAT can be as simple as buying a book by Princeton Review for about $20. It's all the investment you need to save many thousands of dollars on the cost of college.

If your child is social and learns best in groups, they might not accept studying in their home easily. It may make sense to enroll them in an SAT prep class at a test prep center. If you find your child does better with guided test preparation, look up Kaplan or Princeton Review classes. They often offer free evaluations, hoping your child will take the free evaluation and they'll be able to talk you into the class. Even if you're not interested in enrolling your child in a class, it can be helpful to go to Kaplan or Princeton Review for their SAT and ACT assessment tests, because they're giving a free opportunity to experience a live test situation.

Remember, your child doesn't need a perfect score to get big scholarships; all they have to do is improve their own personal score. If your child begins with lower-than-average SAT scores and they study hard, they will likely be able to raise their scores to above-average. This can still make an enormous difference in your cost savings. A scholarship is not out of reach if your child isn't an academic superstar!

Other Outside Documentation

SAT Subject Tests, AP, or CLEP tests are other effective ways to document your student's academic ability. You can also include outside documentation from any outside classes, including community college, online courses homeschool co-op classes, or any public school course work.

Chapter 4

Stand Out from the Crowd

What kind of student appeals to colleges? What makes them offer big scholarships?

Colleges don't want cookie-cutter applicants; they want students who look different and stand out in a crowd. The way to accomplish this is to allow your child to dig into their areas of specialization. Encourage their interests as much as you can and cover the core classes. Of course, they should not spend so much time on their specializations that they don't have time to cover core classes; there does need to be some balance!

If you're not sure what your child's passion is, what are you always telling them to put down when they're supposed to be doing schoolwork? Usually, this indicates their area of specialization.

Colleges want students who are unusual and have real character, so encourage your child to engage in outside activities. When we were homeschooling high school, we focused on academics four days a week, and on the fifth day, it was time for our sons to specialize. Granted, on that fifth day they needed to get their math done to be able to finish the book in a year, but the fifth day was when they also worked on what was particularly interesting to them. One of our sons spent time studying and reading books about economics and history. The other son studied and worked on his chess.

Later, they both got jobs in their areas of specialization. One was a chess teacher at local public and private schools, and the other got a job at a think tank discussing and helping write books about economics. They each had a day each week to devote to their specializations. This gave them something unique that helped them stand out from the crowd when it came time for college scholarship competitions.

Your child could take their specialization and turn it into a real job or engage in some significant volunteer work. Anything that can make your child stand out is important when it comes to earning non-academic scholarships, and even scholarships based on academics. It can be especially helpful for your child to stand out in non-academic areas if they're less academic than their peers.

Chapter 5

Letters of Recommendation, Reading Lists, and Community Service

When it comes to earning scholarships, letters of recommendation are important! Some homeschoolers say you should be collecting letters of recommendation like they are Monopoly money. This is not true! Letters of recommendation are only useful when they are current and are sent directly. A stack of recommendation letters won't do your child much good unless they're getting those letters to colleges. And colleges usually limit letters of recommendation to three, which eliminates letters your child has been collecting since 9th grade.

When preparing recommendation letters, there are some basics you need to remember. It's helpful to get recommendations from people who are familiar with your child's area of specialization. For instance, if your child has a home-based business and does the bookkeeping for your lawn maintenance business, then the person who taught her how to use the QuickBooks software in the past can write a letter of recommendation, saying, "Susan was so quick in learning QuickBooks and she far exceeded the class. She's never had any difficulty, and I've seen her do some QuickBooks for a home-based business." This will show your child's specialization and give a broader picture of who they are to colleges.

The two most important things to remember for a letter of recommendation are that the person must know your student well and must be able to write well. Because a non-family member usually writes a letter of recommendation, you may not know how well that person writes. When our sons were seeking letters of recommendation, they asked our pastor, one of their coworkers, and a professor at the university to each write one.

To determine if somebody can write well, try reading the emails they send, what they write on Facebook, or their Christmas cards. If you've seen any correspondence from them, it can help you determine whether they don't like to write or if they write poorly (in which case no matter how well they know your child or like them, they won't be an appropriate choice for a recommendation letter)! Find people who write well, and who know and love your child, and you'll find great recommendation letters!

I like to tell the story about my best friend's son, who always struggled with tests. His letters of recommendation were so strong that he was admitted to a university engineering school with an excellent scholarship, even though his community college grade point average was quite low. Letters of recommendation can be the outside documentation needed if test taking is not your student's strength.

Reading Lists

In addition to recommendation letters, it's important to include a reading list with your child's college applications. Colleges want to get to know your student, and providing a reading list tells them a bit more about the student's interests and specialization. It also gives clues about your child's reading level, how much they can get done, how fast they can read, and what they read for fun.

Several colleges have told me they want to see students with a wide variety of reading interests. Some colleges get frustrated with homeschoolers who only read classical literature. They prefer students to mix it up, with some books from a reading list for the college bound and some popular literature such as best sellers or popular books that are in the news. Make sure your student's reading list is broad, and doesn't consist of only one genre.

Community Service

Of course, every parent wants their child to be a well-rounded individual with work, community service, and leadership experience. This is especially important when it comes to college and scholarship applications. Every college looks favorably on community service. But remember, nobody can do it all!

I'm not a perfect person and my homeschool wasn't a perfect homeschool; we weren't perfect, yet my sons earned full-tuition scholarships.

Although we did cover a lot of academics, my children also got a lot of work experience (because one day a week they worked at jobs involving their passion and delight-directed learning). But they didn't have much community service experience. When colleges asked us how many hours of community service our sons had completed, I was embarrassed, because I spent a lot of my own time on community service but my children had volunteered little. We had to think hard and count every hour they'd served, because this was a weak area for them.

Nobody has it all. Strive to get your child experience in community service, leadership, and work. But if you don't have every single piece, don't panic!

Chapter 6

Homeschool Records and Course Descriptions

Listen. You don't have control over everything about your child. You can't always make your child write well, test well, get a job, or suddenly become an extrovert.

But there is one thing *all* parents can control. You can provide outside documentation with thorough homeschool records.

Comprehensive homeschool records include:

1. Official transcript

2. Course descriptions

3. Reading list

4. Activity and award list

5. Work samples

6. School profile and counselor letter (may be requested by colleges)

When you're looking for big college scholarships, it's important to provide excellent homeschool records. Start early! Always be prepared. Keep those records updated.

Create a transcript and write course descriptions each year. This is the part of the scholarship process that you have the most control over as the parent. You can't control their study skills or performance on the SAT test. But you *can* control the homeschool records. You *can* make your child's academic record stand out above the crowd.

The student who doesn't have a care in the world about the cost of college may do well by merely submitting an SAT score and a transcript. It's possible to be accepted to a college this way. But for most students, it's not only about getting into college, it's about being able to afford college. Therefore, most people need more than the minimum transcript and scores. These are important—the content of the transcript matters a lot. But your child also needs course descriptions (including some grading criteria), because they give more information about your homeschool to colleges.

Essentially, when a college awards a scholarship, they're placing a bet that your child will be successful in their school. They are investing in your child, based on their confidence your child will succeed at college. The more you can convince them your child will succeed, the more money they're likely to give. Providing course descriptions and grading criteria will explain and demonstrate the rigorous quality of your homeschool.

When creating course descriptions, provide the texts you used, as well as any educational experiences or supplemental work. Keep careful records and format them in a way that makes sense to the college your child is applying to. If you can, contact the college and say, "I'm a homeschool parent and I want to provide my child's information in a format that works best for you." Then submit your child's information exactly how they want it.

In our homeschool, I took an example of my course descriptions and gave it to the college admission office. I asked if they would like to see course descriptions and they said, "Yes." I showed them the example, told them I had this much information for every homeschool class and asked if this was what they wanted to see. And they said, "Yes" and, in fact, went farther than that. The admissions officer said, "I wish that every public high school student had course descriptions like this, because so many kids are coming to college and they can't write at a college level." Keep careful records and provide them in a way that colleges will appreciate.

See the Appendix for more on course descriptions.

Chapter 7

College Fairs and Visits

The search for big scholarships has a lot to do with finding the *perfect fit* college. An academically average student who applies to Harvard will find it difficult to get in. Harvard won't be a perfect fit college for them, because Harvard turns down thousands of 4.0 applicants every year. But when you find colleges where your student will be admitted and valued—perhaps because of their ability to play a certain instrument, or excel at a certain sport, or because of their cultural background or affinity for math—those colleges will do everything they can to woo your student, because your student will be a perfect fit for the school. The question then, is how do you start finding perfect fit schools?

College Fairs

The first step is to go to a college fair. These usually run in the fall months of September, October, and November, while some are even held as early as August. If you search my website for college fairs, you'll find all the resources you need for tracking them down, or you can do a Google search, type in the name of the city that's closest to you and the words "college fair."

When you go to the college fair, talk to each college, and tell them about your child. Tell them about your child's area of specialization and what they're interested in learning about and doing in future. This will help you figure out which college your child will be interested in, and which colleges are interested in your child. They will ask for your address so they can send you marketing materials. I think it's helpful to give them your address so you can start receiving college packets, because it's through these publications you can learn how they allocate scholarships.

In addition, you should visit each school's website, to see whether they have special musical or sports groups your child might be able to try out for or join. I know one family who found a college desperate for a concert pianist; the student was given a full-ride scholarship to attend because of his musical abilities! He was a perfect fit for the college, and the college was a perfect fit for him.

College Visits

Visiting colleges is a critical part of your student's college decision. While it is an investment of money and time, it will save you money in the long run. There's nothing worse than sending your student off to a college they have never visited before, only to discover there is some key element which drives your student crazy that wasn't apparent on the glossy, four-color college brochures. Your child will be spending the next four years of their life at this place, so making sure they like it first is wise, even if it can be somewhat costly.

When you visit colleges, don't forget the importance of taking notes. It's important to get as much personal information about each college as possible. When you apply to the college, your child will be able to use all those personal details in their essays, email communications, and thank you follow up notes.

For example, my son sat in on an honors program class when we were on a college visit. When it came time to write his college application essay, he wrote, "I want to go to SPU because when I heard Dr. Reinsma speak on the core relation between French literature and Italian Renaissance ornate architecture,

I wanted to." Make sure you include as many details in your college visit notes as possible, so your child can incorporate them into future communication with the school. Schools keep track of the number of times you contact them, and they will be favorably impressed to see that you were paying close attention to them during your visits.

When you do find that perfect fit college, make certain to carefully compare financial aid offers, because those offers will come in over an extended period, and you will want to find the one that is best for your bottom line. One college may say, "We'll give you $25,000 worth of scholarships," but if the college costs $36,000, you will still be out $11,000. Another college may say, "We're going to give you this much financial aid," but all their aid is a grant that you don't pay back. Compare this to the college who may give you more financial aid, but it's all in loans your child must pay back.

And don't forget to factor in all the little incidentals for each college, such as ASSP fees, parking fees, or technology fees, as well as travel home on breaks. Sometimes these details will tip the scales in favor of one college over the other.

Aiming Low vs. Aiming High

For the bigger scholarships, students should aim low, which means searching for colleges that make them look like a genius in comparison to all the other applicants. Some people might say that your child should apply to a more challenging school, and they certainly have a point. But when you need help paying for college, it sometimes means not aiming for the most rigorous college, but for the one that will award your child with the best financial aid.

The perfect fit college is the one for which your child compares well with the other applicants—their test scores are better than everyone else's. Even if your child's scores aren't perfect, though, if they're better than the other scores, they will stand out. In addition to being the best qualified applicant the college will see that year, you also want to convey to the school that your child wants to attend; the college won't be tempted to give scholarship money if they sense the student wouldn't go to their school even if offered an excellent scholarship.

Compare your student's SAT or ACT scores to the school's average incoming freshman SAT or ACT score, which you can find in a variety of books that compare college statistics (such as the "US News and World Report College Guide"). Even as you aim low, make certain that your child is truly interested in attending the school, and that they have the strengths you are demonstrating. Make sure you're honest at all costs, because it will all find you out later. Don't let your child say that a school is their number-one school if it isn't. Even if it's not their first-choice school, you can still show the school you love them.

Another strategy is to aim high. Once you have found a college that will make your child look like a genius, aim high within that college by choosing an in-demand field of study. Fields such as math, science, and engineering offer excellent scholarships. Nursing programs offer great scholarships; it is an in-demand field. If you happen to have a daughter who excels in math and science, engineering schools are dying for female students. There are few young women applying to get into engineering schools. If your student is interested, try to stretch your child to a major which the college will value and desire.

Chapter 8

Comparing College Statistics

Your student is interested in both the local public university and the expensive private one across the country; which one is cheaper? When it comes to comparing colleges, it's important to remember that the financial differences between attending a private school and a public school are negligible.

Most public schools are tied to the state's money, and the cost of public university is going up while the number of scholarships is going down. Meanwhile, many private schools are doing well and may offer huge scholarships. Even though their sticker price might be overwhelmingly large, the amount that students pay to attend is significantly smaller.

After you've decided which colleges you and your child think you might want to visit, get out the college guide and look over each college. Start by looking up the average SAT score for each college. Usually it will show the percentage of applicants who have test scores at a certain level and what the average score is. Look for colleges where your student's test score is on the high end of average, so that they are one of the smartest students colleges see and the colleges will want to offer them scholarships.

The "college cost as affected by the average number of scholarships awarded" is another piece of information you can find in these guides. Some colleges will state the amount of the scholarship award the average student can expect. Others will state that the average student will graduate with a certain amount of college debt. This information will help you determine how much an average student usually pays in tuition.

In addition, make sure to check the graduation rate, because that will have an enormous impact on the long-term cost of college. For example, at a local university it takes six years on average to graduate. But at the school my sons attended, almost everybody graduates in four years on average. If you had to pay for six years of school, it would be more expensive than paying for four years.

Lastly, evaluate what percentage of students at each school are employed immediately after they graduate. If your child takes on college debt, they want to have a good chance of getting a job so they can pay off the debt. The employment rate is a good indication of their likelihood to get a job immediately after graduation.

At the university my children went to, the professors were careful to make sure every single student had a college internship over the summer. Therefore, their employment rate was high and almost every student got a job after they graduated from school. Compare this to a larger university, where professors aren't as invested in getting internships for their students, or maybe their students don't care about internships. They don't have anything on their resume, don't get a job when they graduate, and can wind up struggling.

Chapter 9

Application Essays

One of the keys to winning big scholarships is to write excellent application essays. The problem with application essays is that they must be technically perfect, self-reflective essays. I know this can be a problem! Technically perfect, self-reflective essays are difficult and can take a lot of time.

Therefore, make sure you have put aside time to get these essays done. One way to do this is to have your child begin practicing application essays when they are a junior - even as the basis for their junior year English program. When they apply to college, they will have a variety of essays to draw from. If you have a senior, I encourage you to hit the ground running on the first day of senior year. Make sure their first writing assignment is a college application essay. Even if they haven't decided what colleges they want to apply to, grab a college essay topic and have your child write.

Colleges often ask for more than one essay, and each one should be a completely different picture of who your student is. Make sure they never repeat anything from one essay to the other. To understand this, imagine yourself standing in a field surrounded by three friends who are taking a picture of you. Each picture is a completely different photo, a completely different side of you, with a completely different background.

This is what you want from each of your child's application essays. For example, one of my sons played chess all the time, but he was only allowed to use the word *chess* in one of his essays. It was difficult for him, and we had to brainstorm ideas for other topics he could write about for the other essays.

Using notes from your college visits can help shorten your child's essay-writing time. If they're applying to four different colleges and you're trying to convince each one you love them, your child can use much of the same information in each essay and simply change some of the details. For example, for one school your student might say, "I enjoyed Dr. Smith's class because he talked about French literature." They can rewrite this same essay for a different college and say, "I enjoyed meeting with Dr. Reed and seeing how he explained micro-economics in a way that I understood." This will make your child's essays personal, without taking a lot of additional time.

College application essays are like scholarship essays, and usually both will ask the same type of questions. Re-using essays is a wonderful way to save time. One essay could be written for a college application and then used later for a scholarship application.

Most essays require the student to answer specific questions, such as, "Evaluate a significant experience or ethical dilemma you have faced and its impact on you," or "Given your personal background, describe an experience that illustrates what you would bring to the diversity in a college community or an encounter that demonstrated the importance of diversity to you." Sometimes students won't have any idea how their experiences intersect with the essay prompt, and they will need your help to come up with ideas.

When our sons were first writing application essays, they had to write on the topic of diversity. They brainstormed but came back with no idea what to write about. My husband and I tried to help them brainstorm all the different possibilities, showed them to our children, and asked, "Which one do you think would be something that you could write on that has to do with diversity?" They chose one thing and began writing.

Sometimes, we understood the questions on the essay prompt slightly differently than our children did. For example, for the question on diversity, my child's initial response was, "I don't have anything to say about diversity because I am a white male." He didn't understand that the college was asking how he interacted with people who were different from him. We could put this in context and reminded him, "You've been teaching chess at the Chinese Academy for three years, and have been dealing with a lot of people who are different, so why don't you talk about one of those stories?" Then he could take it from there.

It's important to remember that essays are written by the student with the student's own voice. Colleges will know immediately if a parent has helped too much. However, parents can provide edits. The process will go more smoothly if you brainstorm the topic, give the topic to your child, have them write it the first time through, and then edit it together. It does have to include perfect grammar and spelling. You might also want it edited again by someone outside the family, to make sure that nothing is missed. Then have the student correct the essay again, incorporating any edits suggested.

For more on application essays, check out my book on Amazon, *College Application Essays: A Primer for Parents*.

Chapter 10

Focus on What's Important

If you're up to your neck in the processes of creating homeschool records, applying to colleges, and looking for big scholarships, remember to focus on what is important, such as faith, character, values, and work ethic. These qualities will help your child truly succeed in the long run. Real homeschooling is about learning; it's not merely about homeschool records. If you do your job as a homeschool parent and focus on the important things, then your records will reflect this and your student will reap the benefits.

Homeschooling gives you a huge advantage as you prepare your child for college and for life. When you homeschool, you can provide a rigorous curriculum that's a perfect fit for your children, no matter what their strengths are. You can allow plenty of time for the specializations that interest them. You can give them any kind of specialization, provide anything that your student wants to learn, improve communication skills, and emphasize integrity and work ethic, which will help them be qualified for jobs and equip them to be successful in the long run.

You can shape and mold your child's character while they're at home, so they will become pleasant adults when they grow up. You have the freedom to choose any kind of outside documentation that works to support their transcripts, whether this means CLEP, AP, SAT Subject Test, ACT, SAT, or letters of recommendation. You can include all their educational experiences on the transcript, and not merely things done within school hours during the school year.

Remember that homeschoolers are like diamonds. When they apply to colleges and for scholarships, you want your student to be the most interesting applicant they see all year. Like a diamond, they measure each one. Diamonds are measured by cut, color, clarity, and carat weight. The cut for a homeschooler is the depth of their character, work ethic, and values and the color is how unique they are. Clarity is how well they communicate and the carat weight is the rigorous curriculum and with weighty academics. You are the jeweler for your child, so focus on preparing your diamond for college.

Conclusion

Plan Ahead

Every year I see a handful of sad moms who didn't plan ahead. Don't let this happen to you! One mom had her daughter take the GED so she wouldn't need to create a transcript—then colleges wanted one anyway, and she missed the application deadline. Another mom missed out on scholarships completely and her child was devastated about being unable to afford to attend college. I knew one mom who thought her daughter was going to community college, but her daughter suddenly changed her mind and decided to go to university, leaving her mom scrambling.

One mom had a 28-year-old son who

wanted to go to graduate school and needed a high school transcript and course descriptions, even though he already had a bachelor degree. Another mom I knew developed serious health issues, and her husband struggled to create records alone.

The permanent record is your job. You are educating your child, and the government sees you are a school. All schools must complete paperwork. Most colleges want some proof of education.

The financial reward for this work can be enormous. Most families need money for college and academic rigor is often rewarded with scholarships.

You are trying to convince colleges your homeschool is the *real deal*. They won't take you at your word, they want to be convinced. It's easy to convince *me* about how great your homeschool is in a 20-minute conversation, but convincing colleges takes more work. Colleges are not sympathetic friends. They look for data and verifiable facts and want to see evidence to support your claims. You are not alone—they look for this from public schools and private schools, too. They are searching for well-educated teens, who can be hard to find. Show your unique education in written words and provide comprehensive homeschool records. Colleges want to know all about your school—they want *show and tell* and not only *tell*.

Let me tell you the rest of the story. You remember me telling you that my homeschool records strategy was now being replicated by hundreds of homeschoolers around the country. Let me tell you what happened to one of them ... in her own words. My Gold Care Club member, Traci, "clipped" all the "coupons" available to homeschoolers. It took her *hours*. She said, "I cannot imagine trying to do it on my own," and calculated that even if she spent 100 hours in the process, she was making about $1600 an hour! If you had the perfect job, working from home, loving your children, how much could you earn per hour, do you think? Traci found out that her job as a homeschool parent was earning her *well* over minimum wage. Can you believe it? Working on her child's homeschool course descriptions yielded $1600 per hour in scholarships!

> I just had to write to let you know that my daughter received the Regent's Scholarship for a $40,700 annual award. I am still in shock daily. Of course, this is after hours and hours of work on both of our parts, my daughter writing countless essays and filling out applications, and me writing course descriptions. But we figured out that even if we spent 100 hours in the process, we were making about $1600 an hour! I cannot thank you enough for all the direction you have given me over the past few years. Honestly, the college application process has proven to be

one of the most challenging things I have ever done. It challenged my faith and sanity. I cannot imagine trying to do it on my own. Thank you for choosing to spend your post-schooling years helping others! The prospect of homeschooling high school *is* scary, but looking back, the blessing of intimacy I now share with my daughter by having spent these past four years together was worth it. Thank you for helping!

Sincerely, Traci Minor

Why would you share this information with your spouse? Because writing course descriptions is like changing a baby's diaper. It's a dirty job, but somebody has to do it. If you and your beloved can agree that course descriptions are important, and encourage one another, then maybe you can have the perfect job working from home, too, and earn *enormous* amounts of cold, hard cash for college.

If someone *handed* you $160,000 in cash to do a job for 100 hours, would you do it? You probably would. Traci testifies to how much money "clipping college coupons" can save you . . . a lot more then clipping grocery coupons can! You too can get the big scholarships!

Appendix

How to Write Perfect Course Descriptions

Some colleges say they don't need course descriptions, but most colleges require, request, or appreciate course descriptions. A wise homeschool parent will maximize scholarships by writing perfect course descriptions for core classes, electives, and delight directed learning.

Why Colleges Want Course Descriptions

A student's high school record is the most important factor in college admission decisions. Grades and the academic rigor of classes are even more important than SAT or ACT scores. You see, studies show that the academic rigor of the high school curriculum is the single best predictor of success in college.

Your homeschool course descriptions provide proof that your curriculum is challenging. Course descriptions include details that show how your child succeeded with this challenging curriculum, and earned a solid GPA using rigorous material. This is why you create course descriptions.

You do not have to use a school-at-home curriculum, or provide classroom instruction with outside teachers. Instead, you can continue to provide a normal, natural home education using the curriculum and learning style that fits your child and your family. At the same time, parents can learn to take this awesome real-life education, and transform it into words and numbers in course descriptions that colleges understand.

In my experience, homeschool course descriptions can make the difference in scholarships. Colleges would rather not give scholarships, of course—they don't want to create any impediments to paying full price for college. For this reason, sometimes colleges say, "No, thank you." Sometimes you have to work extra hard to get scholarships. The more information you can provide about your homeschool, the more they understand the value of home education.

If you are ready to get started, I have created a comprehensive tool to help you complete homeschool records quickly and easily, so you can help your child win scholarships. Learn more about the Comprehensive Record Solution here.

Ingredients of Perfect Course Descriptions

When it comes to course descriptions, the more information you can provide about each class the better—as long as you don't go over one page of information. This is why I often suggest that each description include three main ingredients.

1. A paragraph describing what you did

This portion describes the academic rigor of the class, including the topics covered and your study methods.

2. A list of what you used

The list could include textbooks, natural learning, or a mishmash of curriculum. It should include resources you used intentionally, but also things you used accidentally by following rabbit trails or going on field trips.

3. A description of how you evaluated your child

This is the part of the description that shows how the child performed. It should include natural evaluation, and not only tests.

Within these main ingredients, there are many ways to give information about your class. Some parents go into great detail for each one, and others don't. However, it's normal to have one paragraph per section, and one page per class. More than one page per class is too much. If your course description doesn't include a class title and a list of what you used, then it's too little.

Three Writing Prompts for Course Description Paragraphs

The first portion of a course description is a descriptive essay. In other words, it's simply a 5th grade writing assignment. It's true! We taught our 5th graders to write a descriptive paragraph, and we can do it, too. Write this course description paragraph the same way you taught your child to write a descriptive paragraph. Start by using a writing prompt, so you have a framework, and then you can be more creative later, as you become more comfortable.

These three writing prompts will help you describe what you did in your high school course description.

1. "In this class, the student will . . ."

This prompt gives you the verb tense and point of view of the writing style, so you don't get stuck figuring out if it should be past, present, future or past perfect tense.

2. "The student will study _____ with _____."

This prompt helps you focus on what you are writing and why. Fill in the blanks: "The student will study Algebra with Saxon Algebra 1 by John H. Saxon Jr."

3. "Topics include . . ."

This prompt helps you use the table of contents to construct a major portion of your course description. List topics from the textbook table of contents or online curriculum descriptions.

As you are learning to write a course description, I suggest you begin with the easiest course description, such as math, for which you use a textbook. Then you can combine all the descriptions together. For example, your description might look like this:

In this class, the student will study the concepts of Algebra 1, using Saxon Algebra 1 by John H. Saxon Jr. Topics include . . . (grab all those freakish math words from the table of contents and insert them here).

Four Ways to Describe Homeschool Evaluation

Teachers in schools usually have 30 or more students to evaluate and need tests to assess learning. Homeschoolers are not hemmed in the same way. Our evaluations can be primarily through natural assessments. We can watch what our children do, evaluate what they know, and grade what they produce.

Homeschool grades should always include a variety of ways of evaluating, but each homeschool parent will have a unique way of describing how they determined a grade for each class, using their normal, natural homeschool process for evaluation.

As you describe your grades, you can give an overview of what you are basing your grade upon, like this simple overview.

1. Overview

Grading criteria: 40% Tests, 40% Daily Work, 10% Midterm, 10% Final Exam.

Or you can simply provide a conclusion with the grade that was ultimately earned, like this example.

2. Conclusion

Final Grade for Algebra: 94% = A

You might decide to give a blend of

overview information and final grade. You could describe what was evaluated plus the final grade.

3. Blend

Grading Criteria: Tests and Exams 60%, Classwork and Homework 40%.

Final Grade for Algebra 1: 94% overall for 4.0

Or you (like me) could provide detailed grading criteria with individual grades and scores for each test, quiz, or paper. This description would list all test scores and all report grades, providing the most detail possible.

4. Detailed Grading Criteria

Here is an example. (Click on the image to see it full size.)

When I wrote course descriptions, I tried to provide every possible individual grade I could within a grading table. I wasn't perfect, though. Some tests, quizzes, and lab reports I simply lost, and then I either left them blank or didn't mention they were missing—as if I'd intentionally not used that test on purpose.

Provide course descriptions any way you can—short or long, whatever works. I think any way that you decide is fine, and the more information you can provide the better.

Six Tips for Tough Course Descriptions

Getting course descriptions done can seem overwhelming, but it doesn't have to be! Follow my six steps listed below, and you'll be on your way to completing them in no time.

1. Cut and paste

Cut and paste is much easier than compose and create, so use descriptions from others when you can. This is why I provide hundreds of course descriptions in my Comprehensive Record Solution. Within the Course Description Collection, you can use "Control-F" to find the specific description you need.

2. Copy from products purchased

You can copy descriptions from course curriculum providers you have paid to purchase their curriculum. You can also copy from books of high school course descriptions. If you own my book, Setting the Records Straight, you have my permission to use the course descriptions in it. You can also use your own curriculum suppliers' course descriptions.

3. Avoid plagiarism by using the Starbucks Method

You can avoid plagiarism when writing course descriptions by first learning and understanding the course description, then rewriting it in your own words. I call this "The Starbucks Method." Read the descriptions. Sip your latte. Nibble your cookie. Spin around three times in your chair. Then write the description in your own words, so it sounds like you. Remember, you don't have to worry about plagiarism if you purchase my book, Setting the Records Straight, or my Comprehensive Record Solution, because you have my permission to use the course descriptions in these resources, as written. You only need to modify them to fit your own grades.

4. Describe delight directed learning

Include course descriptions for delight directed learning. These classes are neither less important nor more important than textbook learning course descriptions. Course descriptions are important for every class - they are not more important or less important for physical education, occupational education, or math. Particularly when you are compensating for average test scores, you want to show the rigor of your homeschool classes through these course descriptions. They can include the various hands on activities for each class, such as field trips, workshops, and jobs.

5. Imitate a school syllabus

There is nothing new under the sun, and no matter how unusual your class may be, chances are there is a high school somewhere in the United States offering a similar class. Fortunately, we have a special, scientific "Magical Look Up Machine" called Google. When you are truly stumped, search for the keyword, such as "ranching" and add the words "high school course description" or "high school syllabus" to find a similar class. Then imitate their words and review their grading criteria for ideas (if you didn't grade the class as your child was engaging in the delight directed learning).

6. Cover letters explain unusual situations

Use a cover letter to introduce or explain tough situations you don't want to include on the transcript or in the course descriptions. My cover letter was a simple introduction. "Enclosed are the comprehensive homeschool records for my son, Kevin Binz." But a cover letter can be your best friend if you need to explain complicated situations, such as taking five years to finish high school, health troubles, failing grades, or changes in school situations.

Perfect Record Keeping Not Required

Perfect record keeping means keeping records, including creating course descriptions. It does not mean you have perfectly kept, tidy records. You don't have to be perfect, grade everything, or even continue the same curriculum for a full year. Beautiful notebooks aren't required either, if simple lined paper or leftover graph paper will suffice. You don't have to always use the same colored pen or pencil or even include test grades in every subject.

You can see from the image provided what my own record keeping looked like, when I was in the middle of a school year. Look closely and notice a few things about my sample on the right. (Click on the image to see it full size.) I spelled "Reading" wrong. My children did so poorly on reading tests, I stopped giving them. I only graded three subjects that year: math, foreign language, and history. In fact, every year I only graded with tests when the curriculum came with tests. I never used a specific pen or pencil. You can almost see my monthly mood swings on each entry.

But, can we discuss the results for a moment? Even though my records weren't perfect, I used them to create transcripts and course descriptions. My children still graduated. They still got into and succeeded in college! They managed to get marvelous scholarships, too.

Perfect record keeping isn't about keeping records perfectly. The homeschooler with the prettiest records doesn't win. Perfect record keeping is just doing it. Simply be sure you are keeping the records. When parents are finished homeschooling their children, what I hear most is not "I wish I wouldn't have done that," or "Wow, that was a huge pain!" What I hear most is shock and awe! Parents are shocked at the wonderful results and amazed at the family closeness.

Course Descriptions Earn Scholarships

Kristen started out thinking, "Could this seriously become a reality for us?" and ended up with a full tuition scholarship.

During the first webinar of yours that I ever joined when my daughter was a freshman, I learned that your sons received full tuition scholarships to their top choice university. I asked myself "Could this seriously become a reality for us?" In the fervent hopes that it could, I devoted months of my time to capturing our daughter's amazing high school education. I closely followed your advice from webinars, the Total Transcript [Solution] and Comprehensive Record Solution, and e-books on how to how to best piece her educational picture together. It paid off! Our daughter just learned that she was awarded a full tuition scholarship to her top choice university, too! A thousand thanks to you and the help that you so graciously provide! ~ Kristen (Minnesotan mom living overseas)

She was not alone in her success. Sharon wrote to me to share the big scholarships that her daughter received.

My daughter was offered a total of

$232,000 in scholarships at this time. We followed all of your tips about course descriptions. Rachel has done a lot of independent learning and had many different interests. That was reflected in her transcripts. I will say the colleges loved the course descriptions. I had someone tell me the colleges did not want all that information but it made a difference for her. ~ Sharon in Texas

The National Association for College Admission Counseling, NACAC, emphasizes the importance of taking challenging classes. "Year to year, we find that getting good grades in challenging courses is what college admission offices value most when reviewing applications from first-time freshmen," said Joyce E. Smith, NACAC's chief executive officer. "Performance in core classes is especially significant, with 79.2 percent of institutions attributing 'considerable importance' to grades in college-prep courses."

Students should take a balanced load - one that allows them to devote the necessary time to each class, because colleges look for quality, not quantity. According to Dan Saracino, former assistant provost for enrollment at the University of Notre Dame, "Nothing is more important than the quality of the course load."

So how do you convince colleges of the academic rigor of each class? And how do you show your child's performance in your rigorous class?

Course descriptions are the answer. I hope this helps you think through course descriptions and why they're important to your child's college admissions packet.

Unfortunately, you have to do the work of writing course descriptions to help earn your child the scholarships. I would love to help you with this task. You know how homeschool parents think about their children's learning styles? Well, I think about your learning style! So, if you would like more help with course descriptions, take my free class on Homeschool Records that Open Doors. If you are super stressed or need a quick read, purchase my easy-reading book on Amazon that describes how to create records, Comprehensive Homeschool Records: Put Your Best Foot Forward to Win College Admission and Scholarships. When you are ready to create course descriptions, you may want to purchase the Comprehensive Record Solution. It includes everything you need from multiple training classes, to templates and descriptions you can cut and paste into your own course descriptions.

Afterword

Who is Lee Binz and What Can She Do for Me?

Number one best-selling homeschool author, Lee Binz is The HomeScholar. Her mission is "helping parents homeschool high school." Lee and her husband, Matt, homeschooled their two boys, Kevin and Alex, from elementary through high school.

Upon graduation, both boys received four-year, full tuition scholarships from their first choice university. This enables Lee to pursue her dream job—helping parents homeschool their children through high school.

On The HomeScholar website, you will find great products for creating homeschool transcripts and comprehensive records to help you amaze and impress colleges.

Find out why Andrew Pudewa, Founder of the Institute for Excellence in Writing says, "Lee Binz knows how to navigate this often confusing and frustrating labyrinth better than anyone."

You can find Lee online at:

HomeHighSchoolHelp.com

If this book has been helpful, could you please take a minute to write us a quick review on Amazon? Thank you!

Testimonials

Amazing Support

I received so much wonderful help and support from Lee over the years. I'm pleased with how the whole home school journey has turned out. Our oldest son, Daniel, is currently a junior in Mechanical Engineering at University of Cincinnati, our daughter, Pearl, is a sophomore in nursing working toward a BSN specializing in Women's Health at Christ College and working as a PCA at the Christ Hospital.

We would not be where we are without Lee. She was an amazing support to us in some of our MOST CHALLENGING times of our family lives. We thank her for all her wisdom and support.

~ Maria in Ohio

Lee Binz is the First and Last Name in Homeschooling High School

Lee Binz is quite literally the first and last name in homeschooling high school. Among Lee's numerous offerings for parents of high schoolers is one that will, I am sure, cause a huge sigh of relief: a transcript solution. There is a 30-day money back guarantee on all of Lee's products.

If you're anything like me, you're not worried about the actual teaching of your child in high school, it's the bureaucratic sundries that keep you up at night. What Lee does is take all that worry off your plate. She has literally anticipated every one of your transcript needs and provided for it. I am being utterly sincere when I tell you that everything you are getting in Total

Transcript Solution is the real deal. It's all genuinely useful, and none of it is fluff or filler. If you have any reservations about creating a college-acceptance gaining and scholarship-winning transcript, this product will allay your fears. More than that, if you are the kind of person that knows that there are things you should have on your radar when you homeschool a high schooler (like the PSAT), you should really consider Lee's products. She is your mentor as you homeschool your high schooler.

That mentorship even extends as far as a phone call. When you buy Total Transcript Solution, your purchase entitles you to one free 20-minute phone consultation with Lee herself.

Truly, if you're homeschooling a high schooler, and will need a transcript at some point, you can't go wrong with this program. While it is true that anyone can generate a transcript with a word processor, it is not true that just anyone knows what colleges are looking for. Further, Lee offers so many choices with her transcript downloads. She shows you what they look like blank and filled in. They look completely professional. There is nothing homemade looking about them. Now, I'm reasonably intelligent and well-educated. I know my way around a word processor. However, I could never have come up with a document that looks this good. It looks like something you paid to have professionally done. I've lost sleep thinking about my four kids' transcripts, but that's one thing that won't be keeping me up anymore.

I'm obviously an enthusiastic fan of Total Transcript Solution. It fills a much-needed space in the homeschool market. It's one of those "Yes, you could do it yourself, but why when someone else has already done it so much better" products. Anything that makes homeschooling high school easier is a big win in my book.

~ Laura from The Old Schoolhouse Magazine

For more information about my **Gold Care Club and the Total Transcript Solution,** go to:

GoldCareClub.com
TotalTranscriptSolution.com

Also From The HomeScholar...

- The HomeScholar Guide to College Admission and Scholarships: Homeschool Secrets to Getting Ready, Getting In and Getting Paid (Book and Kindle Book)

- Setting the Records Straight—How to Craft Homeschool Transcripts and Course Descriptions for College Admission and Scholarships (Book and Kindle Book)

- TechnoLogic: How to Set Logical Technology Boundaries and Stop the Zombie Apocalypse

- Finding the Faith to Homeschool High School

- College Launch Solution (Online Training, Tools, and Coaching)

- High School Solution (Online Training, Tools, and Resources)

- Total Transcript Solution (Online Training, Tools and Templates)

- Comprehensive Record Solution (Online Training, Tools and Templates)

- Gold Care Club (Comprehensive Online Support and Training)

- Silver Training Club (Online Training)

- The Easy Truth About Homeschool Transcripts (Kindle Book)

- Parent Training A la Carte (Online Training)

The HomeScholar Coffee Break Books Released or Coming Soon on Kindle and Paperback:

- Delight Directed Learning: Guiding Your Homeschooler Toward Passionate Learning

- Creating Transcripts for Your Unique Child: Help Your Homeschool Graduate Stand Out from the Crowd

- Beyond Academics: Preparation for College and for Life

- Planning High School Courses: Charting the Course Toward High School Graduation

- Graduate Your Homeschooler in Style: Make Your Homeschool Graduation Memorable

- Keys to High School Success: Get Your Homeschool High School Started Right!

- Getting the Most Out of Your

Homeschool This Summer: Learning just for the Fun of it!

- Finding a College: A Homeschooler's Guide to Finding a Perfect Fit

- College Scholarships for High School Credit: Learn and Earn With This Two-for-One Strategy!

- College Admission Policies Demystified: Understanding Homeschool Requirements for Getting In

- A Higher Calling: Homeschooling High School for Harried Husbands (by Matt Binz, Mr. HomeScholar)

- Gifted Education Strategies for Every Child: Homeschool Secrets for Success

- College Application Essays: A Primer for Parents

- Creating Homeschool Balance: Find Harmony Between Type A and Type

Zzz...

- Homeschooling the Holidays: Sanity Saving Strategies and Gift Giving Ideas

- Your Goals this Year: A Year by Year Guide to Homeschooling High School

- Making the Grades: A Grouch-Free Guide to Homeschool Grading

- High School Testing: Knowledge That Saves Money

- Getting the BIG Scholarships: Learn Expert Secrets for Winning College Cash!

- Easy English for Simple Homeschooling: How to Teach, Assess and Document High School English

- Scheduling—The Secret to Homeschool Sanity: Plan You Way Back to Mental Health

- Junior Year is the Key to High School Success: How to Unlock the Gate to Graduation and Beyond

- Upper Echelon Education: How to Gain Admission to Elite Universities

- How to Homeschool College: Save Time, Reduce Stress and Eliminate Debt

- Homeschool Curriculum That's Effective and Fun: Avoid the Crummy Curriculum Hall of Shame!

- Comprehensive Homeschool Records: Put Your Best Foot Forward to Win College Admission and Scholarships

- Options After High School: Steps to Success for College or Career

- How to Homeschool 9th and 10th Grade: Simple Steps for Starting Strong!

- Senior Year Step-by-Step: Simple Instructions for Busy Homeschool

Parents

- How-to-Homeschool Independently: Do-it-Yourself Secrets to Rekindle the Love of Learning

- High School Math The Easy Way: Simple Strategies for Homeschool Parents in Over Their Heads

- Homeschooling Middle School with Powerful Purpose: How to Successfully Navigate 6th through 8th Grade

- Simple Science for Homeschooling High School: Because Teaching Science isn't Rocket Science!

Would you like to be notified when we offer the next Coffee Break Books for FREE during our Kindle promotion days? If so, leave your name and email below and we will send you a reminder.

HomeHighSchoolHelp.com/ freekindlebook

Visit my Amazon Author Page!

amazon.com/author/leebinz